Twenty-Two Prayer Poems
for Care Givers

Inspired by A Course In Miracles® and Other Sacred Teachings

Fare Thee Well,
Amy
in All ways -
for All ways
"Always"

Twenty-Two Prayer Poems
for Care Givers

Inspired by A Course In Miracles® and Other Sacred Teachings

Donna Iona Drozda

From Wren House • Virginia Beach, Virginia
in cooperation with Natural Press • Manitowoc, Wisconsin

Published by Wren House, P.O. Box 68324 Virginia Beach, Virginia 23471 in cooperation with Natural Press, a division of Natural Ovens of Manitowoc Wisconsin, P.O. Box 730 Manitowoc, Wisconsin 54221-0730

Manufactured in the United States of America

Library of Congress Cataloging-in-Publication Data
        Donna Iona Drozda, 1949-

Twenty Two Prayer Poems for Care Givers
Inspired by A Course in Miracles® and Other Sacred Teachings

Paintings by Donna Iona Drozda

        1. Prayer
        2. Hospice/Grieving
        3. Poetry

ISBN #0-9707676-0-9

To my Beloved "Old Friend" ...
and for
"Nanny" 1908 - 1999

Contents

Acknowledgements

Thanks to the Foundation for Inner Peace in Tiburon, California for making the teachings of A Course in Miracles® so widely available. Appreciation to Dr. Rosemarie LoSasso, Director of Publications, Foundation for A Course in Miracles® Institute Retreat Center in Roscoe, New York for granting permission to use entries from A Course in Miracles®. The Course teaches:

"Nothing real can be threatened.
Nothing unreal exists."

This training remains a constant check and balance for every aspect of the joys and challenges that life has brought my way. Thirteen years into my practice of 'The Course' I was guided by a dream to meet and become a student of The Venerable Khenpo Konchog Gyaltshen Rinpoche, the abbot of the Drikung Kagyu Lineage of Tibetan Buddhism. I am deeply indebted to the vast and unbroken teachings of Tibetan Buddhism and to Khenpo for his beautiful writing, and gentle but powerful guidance regarding the cultivation of Bodhichitta, or Awakened Heart. A Course In Miracles® and the path of Bodhichitta have brought me a powerful blend of East meets West. I am eternally grateful for the tools they each offer assisting me in going H'OM'E to the place of soft heart and inner peace.

Thank you to my angel, Stephanie Erickson, who reminds me joyfully from the other side, to remain comfortably buoyant with change. To Susan Fiori, fellow artist and my inspiration for looking at the art of life in all it's glorious richness. To Barbara Reed Stitt, I bow, she is my friend, mentor and role model. Thanks for all encouragement and support for this project and for a dedication to saving the lives of children. Thanks to B. Joy Davidson, life companion and learning partner as well as the wittiest and most resourceful person I know.

Deep gratitude to my original support group members; Georglanne Kazmir, my spiritual sister, who formulated the idea for the group based upon the work of Jack Boland at The Church of Today in Detroit; Rose Mary Zucker, wise and gentle friend of my soul, who taught me legions about death as she witnessed and worked through her mother's difficult passing and Kathleen Cerveny, exceptional artist, gardener and cultural visionary. Together we learned the art of listening to one another's concerns and aspirations, offering unconditional support for the attainment of our visions and goals.

Thank you to Hospice Volunteers, Inc. of Virginia Beach. The purpose of this organization is to offer support and assistance to families and loved ones as they move through the process of dying. Hopefully, through good care and heartfelt prayer the ending of a life can be an experience imbued with loving kindness, dignity and grace, I dedicate this work to the selfless compassion that they and others like them all over this beautiful planet so freely give to help relieve the suffering of the world.

Thank you to my psychological and spiritual family for their love and support. And precious heartfelt gratitude to my birth son, John Anthony DeKlyen, for your ability to fly like an eagle. "It's so good to see you again."

These prayer poems are addressed to Dear One, Beloved and Old Friend. Dear One and Beloved are greetings for the Holy Spirit, The Great Spirit, within each living being. Old Friend is the name for 'All the yous' that you have ever been throughout time. We are taught that if we call on these parts of our self we will be given guidance and support regarding where to go, what to do, what to say and to whom. Thank you to all these silent Holy Helpers.

Italicized lines in the twenty two prayer poems indicate
quotations or material adapted from A Course in Miracles®

Preface

In 1984 two inspiring doors opened in my life. I became a student of A Course In Miracles® and I began to take part in a circle of spiritual support which has used as its focus these words written by Kathleen Cerveny. I share them as the opening for this meditation collection of paintings and prayer poems written for those who attend to the needs of the dying:

> I am here in the spirit of sharing and surrender.
> I release my will and all the false beliefs
> That stand between me and a fulfilled
> Transformed life.
>
> I forgive everyone who has ever
> Caused me pain.
> And I forgive myself
> For all my mistakes
> Both past and present.
>
> I declare myself a channel
> For Spirit
> For Light
> And for creative energy
> And I gratefully accept
> All that comes to me
> Through this channel.
>
> I ask that honesty
> Insight
> And love
> Be a part of what I share
> With others
> Today.

Twenty Two Prayer Poems for Care Givers came to me while working with my first hospice client, 'Nanny'. She helped me to express as an artist using a new medium; what I call 'the art of compassion'.

Several years ago things had fallen apart in my life. I stood on one of those edge places where it is said that we shatter and then God comes out. Looking back I can see that there were three main aspects of my daily life that allowed me to maintain my center of balance while journeying through that particular 'dark night of the soul'. These three, like the mystical elements in a fairy tale, are my Spiritual practice, remaining close to nature, and creating in my studio. Within this collection of paintings and prayer poems I have combined my three touchstones. My intention for gathering together these painted inner landscapes and centering words is to share a meditative focus for difficult times.

"...each of us has a complete poem somewhere within our soul.
This inner poem is only partially expressed in what we say and write.
... I would say that each of us has a prayer within, a genuine voice of the heart,
but one we never express completely. In our restless desiring, isolated syllables
and even phrases of that beseeching voice can be heard..."

The Silence of God-Meditations on Prayer
James Carse

Once upon a time I took myself on a journey to Tibet. There I was introduced to the remnants of a culture based on more than 2500 years of developing loving kindness and compassion toward oneself and for the benefit of all living beings. Tibetan Buddhism, in its essence, teaches that all living beings were once our mother. A beautiful Tibetan Buddhist prayer illustrates this.

The Four Immeasurables

May all mother sentient beings, boundless as the sky,
have happiness and the causes of happiness.
May they be liberated from suffering and the causes of suffering.
May they never be separated from the happiness
which is free from sorrow.
May they rest in equanimity, free from attachment and aversion.

My journey to the rooftop of the world was difficult and eye opening. It made a deep impact upon my soul. Returning to my home in the Midwest, I sold many of my belongings and relocated to the eastern shore of Virginia. I was blessed to have this be a wonderful adventure supported emotionally and psychologically by three dear friends. However, once in my new life I soon realized that there was to be no comfort zone. It felt as though there was no ground under my feet. It seemed whatever I touched fell away and fell away and fell away, leaving me ever on that edge where, I discovered, we do indeed meet The Divine. I remained willing, day after day, to see my situation differently. As part of this learning I focused upon the idea that I could relax, rebuild, even reinvent, my creative life. I felt as though I had no color, no language, no form, nevertheless I continued to draw and paint as I watched my life shatter around me like a fragile glass.

In the midst of this falling and shattering there was a gentle part of myself deep in my core which emerged with a quiet, motivated courage and strength. It was the giving part. This part patiently and persistently rose up to bring me to the realization that I have a deep love to share.

During this experience I was taught to think of love in broader terms. Now love was to be seen and sensed and felt as an energy. A universal energy of exchange for the benefit of all touched by it. I was instructed from within to practice carrying no more personal agendas. Simultaneously I was guided to become a hospice volunteer. I took action immediately.

Working with my first client, ninety year old 'Nanny', took me into a world foreign to my own. As I have often observed within a powerful and dramatic work of art, it is the contrast that draws the eye and senses into the world which the artist has created. In this instance, I was catapulted into, not only the world of death and the process of dying, but also into Nanny's world of extremely limited means. Suddenly my life was immersed in a contrast that began to open my heart. My life view was transformed. Throughout the year and a half that Nanny and I were together I wrote these twenty two prayer poems. I also wrote down her stories and drew her portrait again and again.

Each creative expression helped me to remain balanced as I witnessed her life sliding further away. These prayer poems are a reflection of the pain and suffering that I felt within the cramped baby blue cement block structure in which Nanny had lived in poverty for more years than she could recall.

During this final chapter of Nanny's life her long estranged seventy two year old daughter came back, by way of social services, to be her care giver. These two women were unable to make peace with one another. The atmosphere between mother and daughter was thick with the heat and tension of deep, unresolved hurts and resentment. My heart opened for each of them. They had been made prisoners in a situation from which they could not escape. I saw myself and all of life mirrored within their struggle.

Each time I served as hospice care giver for Nanny I was reminded of these teachings from A Course in Miracles®:

I am responsible for what I see. I choose the feelings I experience.
And I decide upon the goal I would achieve. And everything that seems
to happen to me, I ask for and receive as I have asked.

"If I cannot hear the voice for God, it is because I do not choose to listen."

and

We are here only to be truly helpful
We are here representing Beloved Spirit who sends us
We don't have to worry about what to say or
What to do.
Spirit sends us and directs us.
We can be content to be wherever Spirit wishes
Knowing Spirit goes here with us.
We are each healed as we allow Spirit to teach us to heal.
                                        Paraphrased from ACIM

Introduction

The word hospice originally meant a place of hospitality where those traveling through Europe could stop for rest and refreshment before continuing their journeys. Over the years, hospice has become not necessarily a place, but the name of an interdisciplinary program of care for the terminally ill and their families, Hospice provides palliative (relief from symptoms) care, emotional and spiritual support. The patient, family and care givers make up the unit of care. These services are provided in the home, hospital or specialized care facility. When decisions have been made to have hospice care in lieu of aggressive medical treatment that may no longer be desired or effective, Hospice Volunteers, Inc. may step in to assist in the unit of care process.

As hospice care givers, we strive to enhance the quality of life and preserve the patient's dignity and wishes during their remaining time. The hospice concept of care treats the person, not the disease, and emphasize the quality, not the duration of life.

Hospice Volunteers, Inc. is a non-profit, tax exempt organization located in the Virginia Beach, Virginia area providing care for the terminally ill and their families. Hospice Volunteers, Inc. is set apart from other organizations providing hospice care by never charging for our services or supplies. We are very proud of the fact that we just celebrated our twentieth anniversary of service to the community and that we are available to anyone needing us. Hospice Volunteers, Inc. is an all volunteer organization comprised of a working Board of Directors from all professions, an Executive Director and administrative staff. We are also fortunate to have physicians, attorneys, nurses, social workers, clergy, business executives and many wonderful volunteers helping to make these services available.

We provide a myriad of services, providing the funding for the purchase of needed prescription drugs, durable medical supplies (wheelchairs, walkers, beds and much more), consumables, and have a bereavement program for adults and children. As indicated above, we do not charge for any of these services. Hospice Volunteers, Inc. is totally dependent upon receiving individual and corporate donations and grants to continue this valuable service. If you would like to obtain further information regarding our services please write or call us at the following address:

Hospice Volunteers, Inc.
4663 Haygood Road
Suite 211
Virginia Beach, Virginia 23455

Cordially,
Katherine Healey Herrmann
Executive Director

A portion of the sale of this book is being donated to Hospice Volunteers, Inc.

For more information on Hospice, please visit the following websites:
www.hospiceweb.com
www.bardo.com

Vision

Dear Beloved,

As I go forward into this new day
Surround me with the energy and light of love.
Remind me throughout this day that at any moment
And in any place
I can begin again and give all concerns to You.
Wherever I go and whoever I see
Or think of let me radiate to that one
A wave of light and love and abundance
So that they too feel the radiance of Your support
And so that together we form the threads that weave
A fabric of contentment and care for all those that
Come into contact with us.

Thank You in advance.   Amen

Patience

"Patience is natural to those who trust."

ACIM

Dear Beloved.

I take a deep breath and recall Your presence.

You are my whole mind,
You are my integrated mind
You never leave me comfortless.

As I remember today to calm and gentle my breath
I also open my mind to release any cluttering thoughts.
I open my heart to be there for those that You place before me today.
Wherever I go and whoever I see may I think of this one as
My own opportunity to practice patience.
My own problems pale.
I release and let all things be exactly as they are.
I rest as I trust in You.
Guide me today.

Let me know where You would have me go.
Let me know what You would have me do.
Let me know what You would have me say and to whom.

I ask today for the patience to open my heart and mind to The Highest.
I ask my heart and mind to extend only The Highest.
I ask throughout this day
Moment to moment
Let nothing less satisfy my soul.   Amen

True Wealth

Dear One,

As I go into the world today
Remind me that there is only one problem...fear
And only one Answer...Love.

If there appears to be a lack, a failure, or an inadequacy
Help me to see beyond appearances to the Truth.
I am ready to be changed today.
I am eager to release my grasp upon ideas of limitation.
I call to You to suround my heart, my mind and all of my movements with
Loving kindness and gentle strength.

Throughout this day wherever I go and whoever I meet
Help me to see this one as a Child of the Light...
A son or daughter of the Earth Mother and Spirit Father.

Today, from moment to moment, let me be the one
Who remembers that there is no lack.
I call in my greater good.
I trust that all that is not meant for me will drop away.

I open my heart mind to receive an increase in allowance space.
I allow more love. I allow more lightness. I allow more beauty.
I breathe in the beauty and the wonder and the innocence
That is my true Nature.

I dance and sing and play as part of every aspect of this day.   Amen

Authentic Power

"To give is ever possible, there's no lack in it."

Tara Singh

Dear Beloved,

There are so many ways in which I feel
Insecure and uncomfortable at this time.

Today I ask for the help to remember that
There is only one problem and only one Answer.
Once again, and a thousand times today if necessary
I lay my concerns at Your feet in gentle surrender.

I welcome and remember that You 'will live with me
and You will teach with me if I will think with You'.
At this moment I require all assistance.

I don't seem to remember how to be there for myself
I don't know how to be there for all the others.
So many seem to be needing something from me.
I feel tired and lonely.
Help me to lay aside my dragons, monsters and strange beliefs.

This is a deep and holy instant in Truth.
Today allow me to be gently reminded that
There is nothing my holiness can not do,
As a child of the Light, as a daughter of the Earth.

Thank You in advance.   Amen

Being Free

'Become free. Become free. Become free of attachment.'

Dear One,

Thank You for the ability today to give all of my burdens to You.
You are my whole mind, You are my integrated mind
and You never leave me comfortless.

I am so pleased to have this opportunity to open my mind.
I welcome and remember that You are ever
Closer than my hands and closer than my feet.

Live with me.
Teach with me.
Today I practice thinking with You.

As I move through this day responding to needs and wants
Whether they are my own or those of others near me
Send in the Mighty Companions to surround.
Carry us all as though we are moving down
a quiet path in summer.

All that I am and all that I have I give to You this day.
May I feel the lightness of freedom from
Attachment to any person, place or thing.
You Beloved are my only substance
You Beloved are my only supply
You Beloved are my only support.

I release all and all to You
I rest in equanimity, free from attachment and aversion.   Amen

The Call

"You are my whole mind, my integrated mind. You never leave me comfortless."
Paraphrased from ACIM

Dear Beloved,

As I move into the day before me
I ask for a deep and gentle balance.
I ask for the ability to release my arrogance.
Assist me please in correcting my own mistakes.

I am no longer interested in pouring energies
Out onto areas of emotional insecurity and neediness.
Send in the Mighty Companions and Holy Helpers.
Teach me true responsibility.

As I move through this day I seek to do no harm.
Monitor my thoughts, my words and my actions.
I am willing to take total responsibility for the emotions of my day.
When I am challenged help me remember to use the circumstance
As a path to take me back to You.
When I am confused remind me to give over every aspect of my need to know.

The Call to return to my devotion to The Highest
This is the only Voice I ask to hear today.
May the quality of this day be enriched by true balance.
May all whom I meet feel the energy of calmness.
For today I celebrate my relationship with You.   Amen

Living in the Present

"This holy instant I give to You, be You in charge."

ACIM

Dear One

There are times like this when I feel insecure.
I am willing to see this situation differently.
When I imagine my response to this experience
It seems as though my need to defend
comes up so strongly.
I want others to see me as good and qualified.
I feel like screaming from the rooftop that
I AM OKAY!
And yet I admit that at this moment I wonder
If I have what it takes.

I find my thoughts wandering into the future.
I see the suffering around me and I question:
Will I be able to age in good health?
Will I be surrounded by love and support?
I offer up these fears to You.
I ask for a new view in this present moment.

I ask that You send in all of the Mighty Companions
I ask that They accompany me.
I ask that They drench my thoughts in gentle delight.

Release me from the pain of imagining that I am
not enough.
Settle me into the arms of The Ones Who care.
Allow me the space and the trust to
radiate out a new idea.
Give me the joy of possibility!
Help me to remember Your Teaching.

This holy instant I give to You
For I woud follow you, certain Your direction
Brings me peace.
And if I need a word you bring it to me.
And if I need a thought You bring I to me.
And if I need but stillness and a gentle quiet mind
These are the gifts I will receive of You.
You are in charge by my request.
And You will hear me and answer me..
For You speak for my Creator and
I am my Creator's holy child.

Thank You in advance.   Amen

Harmony and Harmlessness

I pledge to do no harm.

Dear One,

It feels as though I need to protect myself.
It feels as though I am being attacked.
Wherever I go at this time it feels as though
I am an outsider.

I am bereft of hope and I fear that all of my attempts to
Learn to walk in balance are for naught.
I look about me and try as I may to see the beauty
My eyes seem magnetized
To the pain and suffering and ugliness.

Humbly I ask that You
Give me new eyes in this moment.
Remind me that this world is all an illusion.
Remind me that *nothing real can be threatened.*

Teach me to forgive the world.
Teach me to forgive myself.
Show me how to correct my thinking.
Bring me back to balance.

I am willing to step back today and let
You lead the way.
I am willing to be taught...
There is another way of looking at the world.
I am willing to give over my fear.

Again and again throughout this day
I will be still an instant and go home.
I will listen to Your gentle guiding voice.   Amen

To Choose

"I decide upon the goal I would achieve."

ACIM

Dearest Old Friend,

Today I trust Your guidance.
You teach me that *I am here only to be truly helpful.*
Caring is my choice.
Being of assistance is my one true desire.

As I lean into Your arms for comfort show me the way to care.
As I release my need to know outcomes
Show me the way to care.
While I rest in the center free of attachment free of aversion
Teach me how to care.

I am like a child who requires constant quiet support
Teach me how to care today.

Thank You in advance.   Amen.

The Wheel of Life

"Joy is the vocation of my mind. "

ACIM

Dear One,

Today I open my heart and my mind.
I am willing to be helped.

There are so many ways in which I feel inadequate
and yet as I give each of these shortcomings to You
I sense the gift that comes to fill the space where the fear once lived.

I remember that You teach me that
Those who temporarily have more
Help those who temporarily have less.

I vow today to care for those that You place before me.
I recognize that there are no accidents or coincidences.
I realize that the people I meet today are a reflection of my love for You.

When it seems too difficult today
I request that You lighten me up.
Show me the gentle humor.
Grant me the longer lighter view.

Today I open my heart and mind.
Enlarge my capacity for joy.   Amen

Spiritual Strength and Will

"I will live with you and I will teach with you if you will think with me."

ACIM

Dear One,

Today I face the challenge of 'being present'.
Open my heart to the fullest degree possible.
As I go forward I ask to welcome and remember Your gifts.
Let me extend myself to those that I meet.

When I wonder what to say or do
I trust that my words and actions will be under Your
Guidance and gentle control.
When I am met with confusion
I remember that the only response is to reach for the still
Soft space within my heart where You live.

Thank You for all support today.   Amen

Let Go

"I surrender, I release my will and all the false beliefs
that stand between me and a success filled life."   Opening Prayer

Dear Beloved,

There are those moments in the day when my
Self sabotage part attempts to keep me small and whimpering.
Monitor my thoughts, my words and my actions today.

You have directed my path thus far.
Today I give over all of my seen and unseen
Known and unknown efforts to spoil
The opportunities in which I can help,
In which I can add.
I am willing to release my grasp.
I am willing to let go of all need to know.

Just for today I acknowledge
That You never leave
Me comfortless.
Just for today I welcome and remember
All the ways in which You have removed
Obstacles for me all of my life.

Just for today I will to will Thy will.
Just for today I open to receive
A different set of options.
Just for today I lay all of my judgments at Your feet.

Just for today I empty of all my needs to hold fast.
Just for today I trust that You will carry me
As though we are moving down a quiet path in summer.

Just for today I give it all to You.

Thank You in advance for all Your gifts.   Amen

Dying to be Born

Dearest Old Friend,

I wonder why the idea of death of this body
Frightens me. I feel so uncomfortable
With myself when I consider how I will take leave.
Naturally the body breaks down and eventually
It is no more.
Naturally we can not retain a physical existence forever.
Naturally everything is dying from the moment it is born.

And yet I live in this fantasy realm where I deny
Cause and effect, where I act as if I will never 'run out'.
Today I ask to look at my world as though it is
The last day.
Today I am willing to open my heart mind
To my own passing.

As I walk about and come into contact with others today
I ask to welcome each exchange as though it was a
Simultaneous first and last ever visit.

Naturally I require assistance to face death of any kind.
Today I am willing to invest my attention in noticing
The fragile nature of us all in the physical world.
As I open to receive this awareness
I expand my heart to touch those who suffer
Loss and feel unspeakable anguish.

Help me to be free of my own body thoughts today.
Make me available to meet those
That You place on the path before me.
Give me a soft soft soft as a baby heart.
I pray today for whatever You send me
I ask to learn today of the beauty of being free.
Free free free of attachment to the physical. Amen

Waiting

"It takes great learning to realize that everything is helpful."

ACIM

Dear One,

Perhaps You can feel my raw state today.
I am asking that I be released.
I do not know the thing I am.
I don't know where I am.
I don't know how to look upon this world.
I don't know how to look upon myself.

I can feel such a deeply rooted fear of living and dying.
I feel squirmy and unbalanced.
I feel uncomfortable and confused.
I need help.

I am able to remember that You have taught me
That You will live with me
And You will teach with me if I will think with You.
Today I am on my knees. I am surrendering all that I am.
I am surrendering all that I have to You.
I am willing to lean into Your loving and gentle arms.

Teach me to heal.
Teach me to be whole.
Direct me today.
Let me know where You would have me go, what You would have me say
And to whom.
I am aware that this raw state is also a place
Where I can find You and where I can
Trust that You will guide me safely through.

As I make this rite of passage today
I dedicate each Holy Instant to You.   Amen

Laugh Life

"Can you imagine what it means to have no cares, no worries,
no anxieties, but merely to be perfectly calm and quiet all the time?
This is what time is for, to learn just this and nothing more."

ACIM

Dear One,

Once again I stand on the edge of unknowing.
I am willing to be helped.
Today I ask only that You assist me.

Help me to welcome and remember
That there is nothing my holiness
Cannot do as a child of the Light
As a child of the Earth.

This place and all of its problems and concerns
Seems unreal at best and deeply frightening at worst.
Send in all of the Angelic Helpers
Lift me up above the battlefields.

I am here only to be truly helpful.
You have taught me that You
Will live with me and teach with me.
I need only to think with You.

Clear my mind of any clutter.
Lift my spirit and take me home
Where lightness surrounds.
This place can seem so serious.
I get caught in trying to be certain.
I experience such self importance.
Carry me into the atmosphere of joy.

I breathe in the awareness of You being
Closer than my hands and closer than my feet.   Amen

Falling

"Come to the edge."
"No, we will fall."
"Come to the edge."
"No. We will fall."
They came to the edge. He pushed them and they flew.

Appolinaire

Dear One,

When I look into the face of death I want to run away.
I feel so helpless.

What can I do for this one who lies before me?
How can I say any words that mean anything to this one
So soon to depart this world?

I touch a hand that soon will carry no signs of life.
I listen to breathing that is gasping for a hold.
I see a body that is weak and suffering.
I taste an odor in the air that reminds me of the
Path I also walk and I become unsettled
And squirmy and afraid.

Help me to be present for this one today.
Touch in on my fearlessness and gently take my hand.
Listen to my breathing and calm my mind.
See my body infusing the atmosphere with compassion
Radiating from the quiet center of my heart.
Help me taste the sweetness of the sacred
Rite of passage.

It is truly an honor to visit this edge with You beside me.
Thank You in advance for what I will face this day.   Amen

The Sun, the Moon, the Stars

"Twinkle twinkle little star..."

Dear Beloved,

I see and sense and feel the child
That is filled with wonder at this time.

I remember when You taught me that
We are all like library books on loan
From God's library.
None of us know when it will be time for our return.

As I sit with this one who is soon to depart
My thoughts go to the beauty of the chapters
Which You have crafted for this life.

Whenever there was suffering or sadness
You brought relief.
Whatever obstacles or barriers
Presented themselves
You indicated a path to travel.
It is time now for this one to return to You.

Like any good book we wish for a happy ending.
Let this one be tenderly embraced during
This rite of passage.
Hold this one gently in Your loving Light.

I can see the pages turn slowly signaling
'The end' and I weep tears of joy.
For having known this ones story
I can share it until I too am called back
Home to You.   Amen

The Ancestors

"She who we have loved and lost is no longer where she was before,
she is now wherever we are."   Gravestone Inscription

Dear One,

I am with this one who
Now seems so alone
Lying so still before me
I feel that soon the soul will fly.

I feel the presence of the ancestors
Who came before and who now wait
To be reunited in spirit with this one.

Life is so rich and full and wonder filled
And so must be the passage that this one is soon to make.
I recall that You have taught me that
This idea of life and death is all an illusion.

You said think of it all as a dream.
Consider the waking dream
Consider the sleeping dream
Ask often, "Did I dream this?"

You remind me time and again
To not take this place so personally.

This is an opportunity for me to
Practice letting go of my need to
Have things be different than they are.
I will weave a frame of holiness
Around this one and trust that
There is no death
For it is love that brings us here and
It is love that keeps our ancestors alive.   Amen

Let There be Light

"Only Light can come to me and only Light can be here."

ACIM

Dear One,

I am here in a spirit of sharing and surrender.
I release my will and all the false beliefs
That stand between me and a fulfilled
Transformed life.

I forgive everyone who has ever
Caused me pain.
And I forgive myself
For all my mistakes
Both past and present.

I declare myself an open channel
For Spirit
For Light
And for creative energy
And I gratefully accept
All that comes to me
Through this channel.

I ask that honesty
Insight
And Love
Be a part of what I share
With others
Today.

Birth, Old Age, Sickness and Death

"May all mother sentient beings boundless as the sky
Have happiness and the causes of happiness."   Tibetan Buddhist Prayer

Dear Beloved,

You are my Whole Mind
You are my Integrated Mind
And You never leave me comfortless.

Today I ask to welcome and remember
That You are in charge.
You are the direct link
To the Great All in All
You are the boat that I can
Climb aboard and trust to carry me
To the opposite shore.

I am so willing to learn to release my grasp.

I am willing to let You be in charge.
You are my one true friend and You teach me
The way to offer loving kindness and compassion
To the one(s) before me in the day ahead.

We are each born.
We will each hurt and help as we travel
Today show me how to be of the greatest assistance.
Show me how to listen and how to be still.

As I visit with this child of Yours today
Let my preconceived notions drop away.
Make it all new.
Make it all part of the natural process.
Gently, oh so gently, remind me to radiate
Love and lightness and peace to assist my
Brother/ Sister on this most heroic journey of all.   Amen

Dancing on Top of the World

"On with the dance! Let joy be unconfined."   Mark Twain

Dearest Old Friend,

I remember hearing the story
Of the woman who died
And watched as souls on the other side took
Up their assignments for their coming rebirth.

In amazement she observes a joyous
Jumping up and down as one soul
Chooses a life to come
Filled with apparent tragedy and duress

From this she says she learned
To recognize that we have each
Accepted an assignment to fulfill
While in this present physical body.

It was not this woman's time to remain
And so she came back to tell the story of
What she saw and heard and felt.

Today I ask to keep in mind the many stories
That tell a similar blessed view of what waits
To meet each of us as we venture
Onward from this physical world.

According to many accounts we
Have reason to visualize this rite of passage
As taking us each into Fields of Light
Across a rainbow bridge.

Today let me carry this loving image as
I visit with this one who will soon go home again.   Amen

All is Well

Dear One,

This Holy Instant would I give to You
Be You in charge.
For I would follow You
Certain Your direction
Brings me peace.

And if I need a word
You will bring it to me.
If I need a thought
That will You also give.
And if I need but stillness
And a tranquil, open mind,
These are the gifts
I will receive of You.

You are in charge
By my request.
And You will hear me
And answer me,
Because You speak for God
And for God's holy child.

Thank You for everything.   Amen

Paraphrased from ACIM

Epilogue

Death first came to call when I was seven. Grandpa died. Grandpa Drozda had been transplanted from the old country directly into his chair under the Catalpa tree. He had been there all my life, sitting in the side yard or working in Aunt Marge's kitchen on the other side of the wall in the duplex that our families shared. To my young but observant artist eyes Grandpa appeared uncomfortable in his surroundings. During the time leading up to his death he seemed tired and unhappy. He had been widowed years before my life began and in my innocent child state I saw his death passage as a helpful thing for him. I thought he would be less lonely when he went to heaven and met Jesus and the Guardian Angels and Grandma.

I was well trained by the nightly recitation of the prayer,

> "Now I lay me down to sleep, I pray the Lord my soul to keep,
> if I should die before I wake, I pray the Lord my soul to take".

I imagined that, at death, Grandpa's soul must have felt a quality of being set free, at least I wished that for him. I was surprised and hurt when I spoke this out loud and was scolded by my parents for not understanding that death was 'bad' for Grandpa.

In 1959, when I was ten, Mother moved our family. She took us away from the inner city and delivered us to the suburbs. I died inside. My best friend, "Lucky" the dog, didn't get to come along.

The following year my maternal grandparents passed away within months of one another. I watched with curiosity as Mother and her sister's grew very quiet. Death was not openly discussed. I could only sit alone and daydream about the way that the endings of these special lives would affect my own. Mother brought home a new puppy for me and I began taking long walks in the woods with Tippy. I would follow the raccoon tracks to the creek's edge and feel what I was missing.

From my Grandmother, Julia Toth, I learned of quiet dignity, staunch faith, stoic determination and profuse flower gardens. My grandfather, John Toth, gave me gifts of gentle twinkle-eye humor and a deep love of nature. He planted acres of trees which will grow in my heart forever. I missed the beauty and serenity of their country home. They had surrounded me with kindness and a natural aesthetic. When they died it was like a movie that stops before you get to see the end. I was dropped into The Mystery; it was a cavernous loss. A restless intensity grew within me as a result of my own, and Mother's, unexpressed secret grieving. I wandered through the woods as life went into fast forward.

In my nineteenth summer I learned of another kind of death. On the day that our country buried Robert Kennedy I relinquished my newborn son. I placed him into the adoption system of Catholic Charities. While pregnant I wrote poetry and spoke to the idea that when my child was born I would be reborn and my life would be given a focus that could only have come through this profound surrender. I was hidden away from my family and friends during this time and as a result I became a member of what Jungian analyst, Clarissa Pinkola Estes calls "The Scar Clan," a keeper of secret stories.

This rite of passage forced me into a state of total aloneness, I was just beginning to learn that it is in these spaces of separation that the voice of guidance within becomes most clear. The world continued spinning out of control as the Vietnam war escalated. A dark space opened and swallowed me whole. Within several weeks of giving birth I was trapped, overpowered and raped by three monstrous men. It was through this episode that I came to learn the meaning of cruelty and violence in my own war zone. Left petrified and in a state of panic I was unimaginably isolated.

I was no longer given any illusions about there being ground under my feet. Yet even in the midst of this darkest night a door opened. In August of 1968 life brought me the gift of guardian angel and artist, Alice Twitchell.

When I was nineteen Alice was fifty one. Although she would not tell me her story until twenty six years later, she had also endured a penetrating loss. Her only daughter, my age, had died just months before Alice and I met. Silently Alice and I became blood relatives of the "Scar Clan". She demonstrated a quietly disciplined life lived close to the earth and to her art. She taught me, through example, to study yoga and to begin a daily practice of the quieting of my traumatized heart and mind. Through her strength and guidance I retrieved my dream and began the slow and arduous task of learning to communicate and express what truly mattered in my life through the making of art.

Studying the works and writings of the master artists and spiritual teachers taught me that one who is aspiring to live a creative life must "die" at night to be born anew with each day's expression. I learned that we are stepping over the dead bodies of those who have come before us; all our ancestors. Our privilege and responsibility is to hook ourselves onto the front of the chain in order to add our gifts and talents to the whole. I embarked on what came to be a nine year sojourn into discovery. I rebirthed myself by becoming an impassioned student of the arts and Eastern philosophies. I gardened and composted and became aligned with the passage of the seasons in an organic way that fed my art. I learned to let go as nature drops her leaves by beginning a practice that included burning the drawings done yesterday in order to light my wood stove today. I learned during this time the beauty and art of what I have come to know as the intimacy of impermanence.

Joan Miro, the surrealist painter, conveys this message in an earthy way with:

> Every blade of grass has a beautiful soul.
> Courage consists of staying home and close to nature...
> Nature who takes no account of our calamities.

It was 1984 when I read Dr. Gerald Jampolsky's book Love is Letting Go of Fear. He dedicates this beautiful work inspired by A Course In Miracles®:

> To the children of the universe
> Who, by the essence
> of their being, Love
> Bring light to a darkened world
> And lead us to the Kingdom of Heaven

Dr. Jampolsky introduced me to the concept of giving and receiving being the same in the eyes of Love. I was entranced with the idea that to get Love we need only give Love. The study of art and Eastern spiritual teachings continued to serve as my guide as I began to heal the deep psychological and emotional wounds that I had endured. With this repair a deep passion for sharing surfaced. By the time I reached chapter twelve of Love is Letting Go of Fear it became clear that I was ready to become a student of A Course In Miracles®, a three part course of psycho-spiritual study in changing our habitual perceptions which advises:

> Retain your gifts in clear awareness
> as you see the changeless in the heart of change.

Several years into my exploration of A Course In Miracles®, in my thirty-ninth year, I was blessed to be selected a resident of Ragdale, a place for writers and artists to work. Preserving the Howard Van Doren Shaw Arts and Crafts home in Lake Forest, Illinois, Ragdale was established in 1976. In this creative oasis silence is observed throughout the day. This allows an undisturbed solitude for those taking a break from their work to walk in the virgin prairie or to stop for a mid day snack in the communal kitchen. After dusk there is the opportunity to meet and visit the other residents over dinner and throughout the evening. My time at Ragdale was highly productive. It provided me the opportunity to create the paintings which comprise my Night River series. It also gave me ample time and space to sort out the valuable from the valueless in my life.

I looked back into my childhood and discovered inner strengths and treasures that had been layered over by the years. I called them forward to meet me in an act of creative retrospection. I asked myself:

> What matters?
> What do I want to have come of this life?
> What is this time for?

A Course In Miracles® had taught me to place my goal at the beginning so that all assistance could be supplied from what The Course calls our Mighty Companions. I was immersed in the idea of connecting with what had meaning in my life and so I asked my silent angelic forces to help me discover what would now be most beneficial.

As a result of this inquiry I drove south from Cleveland in the autumn of my fortieth year crossing over Cape Fear to get to Pleasure Island where I rented a small cottage on a spit of land in South Carolina. Immediately after moving my studio supplies in the door I fell ill.

A high fever and chills shook my body. It felt as if my cells were literally bringing up to the surface parts of me that were now ready to be released. I was alone experiencing yet another form of death. During this time I faced the trauma of violence and cruelty that had sent my life into a silent panic twenty one years earlier. From deep within my soul I was able to look the perpetrators in the eye and face the rage of being violated. I wailed and clawed the sky. I saw the suffering as suffering. It rattled through me and connected me to all those who have or will ever experience the injustice of attempted soul murder. I then slowly and lovingly remembered, owned, forgave and released the pain with the assistance of Neuro Linguistic Programming®. NLP gave me the principles and process to make deep and lasting changes, taking away the panic attacks that had made me a prisoner of my body since the violence was first experienced. After three days I finally felt free to face the shadowy truth about the role, I too, had played in the unhealthy quality of several primary relationships.

I invested four and a half months in solitude dedicated to this process. I returned to Cleveland with six hundred written pages and sixty five new 'Island Home' paintings. I now had an even greater awareness of what mattered for my life. I felt at home internally.

In the spring I felt the natural urge for a new beginning so I searched for a new studio. My new work space was most unusual. It was located in what had been a high security lock-up ward for women in a state run psychiatric hospital. I was the first person to make use of the cavernous space since the building had been deserted.

The old hospital facility had been closed and the building abandoned eight years earlier. The first floor was now in the beginning phases of renovation. The structure and its ten acre campus were being given new life as a bright, open, state of the art out-patient elder care facility. I was the only tenant on the top (fourth) floor.

The building sat on a high hill with incredible views of sunrise and sunset. I looked out over the trees to University Circle and Lake Erie three miles to the north.

Most mornings I unlocked the high security doors and entered this raw unrenovated space well before dawn. In the darkness I could feel the pain and suffering lingering through the sprawling halls and many rooms. I reflected on how, at any given time, up to thirty-five women would have been heavily medicated and held in this area. The energy of those who had lived there permeated the walls and floors. I could sense death as it brushed against my cheek. I could smell it. These sensations echoed through the space. I imagined that they filtered up out of the emotional and spiritual death experienced by women who could not express their sorrows or their joys. As my fingers traced the names and symbols carved into the wide wooden sills I learned to understand the meaning of, "there but for the grace of God go I". I often stared out through the prison-like window grates to the beautiful long views beyond.

Here in this place I became more intimate with the ways in which we, as individuals must endure losses. I remembered that even as we periodically spiral into swamps of sadness and dark nights of the soul there is at all times light on the other side of our sorrow. There is a quiet joy at all times waiting patiently to embrace us. We are, in truth, crossing over a rainbow bridge to fields of light and we are never left comfortless as we travel. At all times we are surrounded, supported and gently moved along our path by invisible Helping Hands.

I mourned. My heart opened. I danced, jumped rope, roller skated through the halls. As I felt my way deeper into the atmosphere of loss and grieving I painted a series of sensuously alive divers. I imagined them diving into the sea of emotion upon which our lives are seemingly tossed. I visualized these figures diving deep into the healing pool of the unconscious retrieving the lost treasure locked within our individual and collective Wounded Self. I imagined each of us finding our treasure to share with the world. I sang. I hung mobiles from the ceiling that said YES! and NO HARM. I opened the doors of my studio to others who were hanging in the dangle with no ground under their feet. Together we began to playfully create. I painted figures standing in their power with feet firmly planted on the earth, arms stretching up to touch the sky, to embrace the Moon.

A nurse in my Tai Chi class came to visit me. She had worked in the lock-up ward a decade earlier. Slowly, deliberately she spoke of the pain, suffering and medicated isolation which she had witnessed. She was healing herself by telling her story. A former patient of the facility, came back to attend workshops. She told me that the novel The Cracker Factory had been written by a former patient here. She then wandered off during a break to look for the location on the second floor where her roommate had hung herself many years before. She retrieved her own power in the doing and began to sing her own song as a result. A security guard who had moved among the people struggling to hang on said that years later some men who had been made homeless by the closing of the hospital still wandered back to the facility attempting to return to the last place where they had lived. He said they usually return at night, looking for a bed. I imagine that he felt a special gratitude for his own whenever he reflected on this scene.

I learned of many ways that we die each day.

Throughout the five and a half years in the former high security lock-up ward for women I learned that life matters greatly in all its chaos and cherished moments. I created, thanks to the inspiration of powerful teachers in my life, a series of ongoing ritual theater workshops based upon the natural cycles of the seasons and the phases of the moon.

Working with groups in an ongoing creatively intimate manner fed our spirits a diet of what I call "Grace Food". When it was time for me to move on from this old hospital ward I experienced a sense of exceptional lightness and a deep love for the dance of life.

Spiritual practice, remaining close to nature and creating in the studio have gifted me with, what I discovered to be a life long urge to be 'comfortably buoyant with change'. Whenever I feel confused and afraid, whenever I see monsters, dragons and shadows coming to meet me on my path, I ask for help in turning on the light. I may ask hundreds of times a day when necessary!

I attempt to remember what the poet Rumi taught:

> Let the beauty you love be the work that you do,
> there are hundreds of ways to kneel and kiss the ground.

In 1997, after thirteen years studying and practicing A Course In Miracles®, I wondered if I had acquired the ability to live the rest of my life with what The Course calls "joy as the vocation of your mind". As if to confirm my wonder I had this dream:

I am watching as my puppy runs down the quiet, curving street to greet some visitors at a neighbors' home. The guests are three Tibetan monks. They are dancing on the expansive lawn beneath towering trees. My pup happily runs to join them. I retrieve her just as a large white vehicle drives up and seven high Lamas emerge. Everyone is smiling.

My pup has long symbolized joy in my dreamtime so the vision of 'my joy' running down the path to meet ten smiling wise human beings was a delightful confirmation of my wondering.

Within six months of the dream the first formal instructions given by a Tibetan Buddhist teacher came to the area where I live. Listening, I and several hundred others, learned anew of the Buddha's discovery of The Four Noble Truths and the Eight Fold Path:

The Four Noble Truths
1. Life is suffering, for all life ends.
2. The cause of suffering is desire.
3. The end of desire leads to the end of suffering.
4. The way to end desire, and hence to end suffering, is to follow the Eight Fold Path.

The Eight Fold Path
1. Right View (following the Four Noble Truths)
2. Right Thought (caring and unselfish)
3. Right Speech (no lies, abuse or foolishness)
4. Right Action (careful of the feelings and rights of others)
5. Right Livelihood (earning a living which is honorable)
6. Right Effort (out with the bad and in with the good thoughts)
7. Right Mindfulness (keeping heaven in one's heart under all circumstances)
8. Right Concentration (peace as the focus)

I became a student of Tibetan Buddhism. The combination of the instructions of A Course In Miracles®; which teaches that there is no death and the focus of Tibetan Buddhism; which is constantly facing and preparing us for death, provides a blend of psycho-spiritual tools for learning to be 'in the world but not of the world'. I find that when explored simultaneously, this blend of theistic and non theistic world views offers a rich and tranquil fusion of the polarities and contrasts of inner/outer, East and West. By applying these two powerful tools in combination I am able to be present to 'all my relations' in an ever evolving "open the heart" and "open the mind" manner.

In his book *Transformation of Suffering* my teacher Khenpo Konchog Gyaltshen Rinpoche writes:

> Many different religions have arisen to address the attainment
> of inner peace, a universal need which is present in all living beings.
> When faced with a crisis, it is human nature to use all of the
> conventional means at one's disposal in order to resolve it.
> But when none of these work, it is also human nature to turn
> to spiritual practices such as prayer and meditation to help face
> our limitations. At such times, we often learn that happiness and
> satisfaction do not depend solely upon external conditions, but rather
> on the degree of love, compassion, and wisdom that we experience.
> Each of the world's great religions focuses on developing these
> qualities which open our hearts and show us how to live in harmony
> and friendship. They also understand that appealing to enlightened
> beings who possess extraordinary wisdom and compassion, is a
> special technique to ease confusion. With these basic tenets in common,
> religious traditions have developed in various parts of the world,
> each with its own unique practices, methods, and belief systems.
> All of them serve as methods to relieve suffering, pain, and confusion
> and are worthy of respect.

I am now looking on as more of my friends, loved ones and fellow travelers move from this life into The Mystery beyond and it motivates me to look through the open door into the face of death. I am looking at the rainbow bridge.

The twenty two prayer poems that came as I moved down the path with Nanny, each assisted me in feeling and acknowledging the struggle taking place in the thick, hot, heavy atmosphere in which she lived and died. When I first began hospice with Nanny I was most interested in being involved in a program where I could give back. I was interested in seeing love as an energy of exchange rather than as an emotion which takes hostages often unwittingly. I had recently moved through a period of intense emotional drama. I knew instinctively that the way to be clear of all residual effects of the ordeal was to "get over myself" and to, once again, stop taking life so personally. From a quiet place within I was guided to hospice.

Nanny was ninety years old when I became her daughter's respite care giver. Each Wednesday I would arrive at Nanny's baby blue cement block cottage on the Chesapeake Bay. To walk into the dark, dank, airless hot room where she lived as she waited to die was mind altering. I had never actually encountered this particular level of poverty or disconnection with the outer world of time and place. Being with Nanny, listening to her stories and drawing her portrait week after week throughout her last eighteen months helped me to feel deep compassion for the edge of life that we are all approaching.

Each of us will have a unique set of circumstances to face when a loved one passes away. Experiencing the impending death of someone dear to us can be a time when we can benefit deeply by asking for help. This is a time to bring our human insecurities, doubts and fears out of the darkness and into the open light. By admitting to our fragile parts, and learning to first communicate with our Inner Guides and Mighty Companions we can be led to the support in the outer world that will see us through the challenge and difficulty of letting go of those we hold dear. Hospice volunteers around the nation, and the world, are here to aid. Remember in this present moment the Helping Hands surround us waiting for our request to assist. Ask for help.

Donna Iona Drozda
Virginia Beach, Virginia
November 2000

"Forgiveness offers everything I want"

God's plan for saving from loss and harm cannot change,
nor can it fail. Be thankful it remains exactly as God
planned it. Changelessly it stands before us like an open door,
with warmth and welcome calling from beyond the doorway,
bidding us to enter in and make our Self at home, where we belong.'

About the Author/Artist

CR Studio

Donna Iona Drozda is dedicated to creating a 'hand made' life. Her paintings are found in the collections of hundreds of private homes and public spaces and for over twenty years Drozda's images have remained well recognized and enjoyed in her art's community.

Drozda served as Artist in Residence for The Art Studio: Center for Therapy through the Arts, Inc. in Cleveland, Ohio where she created workshops for individuals in life transition and recovery. While there she also developed her mentoring/consulting service, Lifecycle, which assists participants from around the country in becoming more expressively aware of how to create inner peace.

Drozda traveled to Thailand, Indonesia, Nepal and Tibet studying with mystical artists, and spiritual healers. She is a student of A Course in Miracles® and Tibetan Buddhism, whose combined focus is upon the release of suffering for all living beings through the cultivation of wisdom, compassion and the awareness of the impermanence of all things.

Iona gardens, paints and tapes Lifecycle at Wren House Studio in Virginia Beach. Her life mission borrowed from Thoreau states simply that:

"To affect the quality of the day is the highest of arts."

Reference to A Course in Miracles® Second Edition

Resources

A Course in Miracles®, Foundation for Inner Peace, 1975, 1982, 1992, 1999

Love is Letting Go of Fear, Gerald G. Jampolsky, M.D. , 1984

Transformation of Suffering, Ven. Khenpo Konchog Gyaltshen Rinpoche, Vajra Publications, 1996

The Jewel Treasury of Advice: A Hundred Teachings from the Heart,
  translated by Ven. Khenpo Konchog Gyaltshen Rinpoche, Vajra Publications, 1997

The Tibetan Dharmmapada (Sayings of the Buddha), Gareth Sparham, Wisdom Publications, 1986

A Pocketful of Miracles, Joan Borysenko, Phd., Warner Books, 1994

When Things Fall Apart, Pema Chodron, Shambala, 1997

Start Where You Are, Pema Chodron, Shambala, 1994

Tibetan Book of Living and Dying, Sogyol Rinpoche, Harper San Francisco, 1992

The Impersonal Life, Joseph S. Brenner, DeVorss & Company, 1941, 1969, 1986

List of Illustrations

Gi'clee Prints Available.
For more information contact: Wren House Studio
                              P.O. Box 68324
                              Virginia Beach, Virginia 23471
                              (757) 363 0755 Ph/Fax

Visit our website at www.fromwrenhouse.com

donnaisnadrezda.com

The Lifefcycle System by Donna Iona Drozda

Lifecycle is an audio taped 'life energy' consultation.

If you or a significant other are in transition during a period of loss or change in work, relationship, or in other key areas of life you will find that the information brought to you in a Lifecycle consultation clearly communicates creative ideas for opening your heart and mind to a sense of new beginning.

Lifecycle information is delivered to you in a sixty minute audiotape format. Lifecycle provides a blending of information gained from two sources unique to you: a beautiful two page chart of your life energy based upon specific birth information (the color coded charts are included in your order packet) which is compared with an analysis of your handwriting. Lifecycle places a spotlight on the physical, emotional and spiritual areas in your life that could benefit from a tune-up. The one hour tape can be reviewed again and again serving as a highly personalized and useful gift to give to yourself whenever you feel the need to regain balance in your life. The Lifecycle tape serves as an affirmation of those parts of you that are often yearning for a way to wake up and express more aliveness and a more fully creative expression.

****

Lifecycle is a creative service used by hundreds of clients since 1991:

"I continue to listen to the tape you did for me, finding new messages each time. I find your words soothing, uplifting, reassuring and stabilizing and yet exciting and motivating. It was truly a gift!"

~J. B.
Boalsburg, PA.

"A clear January day and I am writing to thank you for your work. I stopped my tape several times to cry for joy! There were several times when your words seemed to rhyme with unspoken words in me. It was powerful and inspiring!"

~S.F.
Long Island, N.Y.

"You did a reading for me about a month ago and I just wanted to say thank you for redirecting my energies in a realistic and positive way. Thank you very much."

~N. A.
Los Angeles, CA.

To Order A Lifecycle Tape:

Send the following:

1. Your name as it appears on your birth certificate (Please PRINT clearly)

_____

First name   Middle name (if there is one)   Last name *(as they each appear on your birth certificate)*

2. Your date of birth: month, day and year. _____/_____/_____

3. A page of your handwriting as you would write everyday. Please put your sample on *unlined* letter sized paper. For content you may write about anything at all just don't use copied or memorized information. Refer to yourself in the first person several times. (i.e. "I went", "I saw")
At the end of your sample write your current legal signature as if you were signing a check.

4. _____   _____
   Name   Email address

   _____   _____
   Street address   City   State   Zip

   _____   _____
   Phone   Fax

5. Send personal check or money order in the amount of $~~140.00~~, plus ~~$5.00 S/H~~.

Send to: Wren House/Lifecycle
     P.O. Box 68324
     Virginia Beach, Virginia 23471

For further information call: 1(757)363-~~0755~~ 7177